Are You as Smart as You Think?

Are You as Smart as You Think?

150 Original Mathematical,
Logical, and Spatial-Visual Puzzles
for All Levels of Puzzle Solvers

TERRY STICKELS

Thomas Dunne Books/St. Martin's Griffin
New York

THOMAS DUNNE BOOKS.
An imprint of St. Martin's Press.

Production Editor: David Stanford Burr

Library of Congress Ctaloging-in-Pubication Data

Stickels, Terry
    Are you as smart as you think? : 150 original mathematical, logical, and spatial-visual puzzles for all levels of puzzle solvers / Terry Stickels; with a foreword by Will Shortz.—1st ed.
        p. cm.
    ISBN 0-312-20911-8
    1. Mathematical recreations.   I. Title.

QA95.S734 2000
793.7′4—dc21   99-088900

10 9 8 7 6 5 4 3

Foreword

To me, nothing beats the satisfaction of encountering a daunting puzzle and, after a real brain workout, being able to come up triumphantly with the solution. In his new book, Terry Stickels offers that satisfaction to readers from the novice puzzle solver to the veteran who demands the most difficult and complex challenge.

Terry and I have been fellow puzzlers for years. He's come up with some of the best stumpers for my radio show on NPR. He has a very nice eye for brainteasers of all sorts, involving words, math, and logic, and has published popular sets of puzzle cards, a puzzle calendar, and other "I dare you to solve this" original creations in a variety of styles.

Now Terry Stickels offers us "one hundred fifty" fine, original brainteasers ranging from easy to hard—something for everyone. Scattered throughout the book are a kind of puzzle traditionally called *rebus*, which Terry has imaginatively renamed *Thinkerobics*. They've been around for centuries, and are many peoples' favorite kind of puzzle—definitely one of mine. They involve artful arrangements of words, letters, sometimes numbers and other symbols, into visual puns on a familiar expression.

For instance:　　　　WORKING
　　　　　　　　　　　TIME

Get it? "Working overtime."

If you're a puzzle person, you've come to the right place. Turn the page and dig in!

—Will Shortz, Puzzle Editor, *The New York Times*

Contents

Introduction

Are You as Smart as You Think? is really two puzzle books in one. The first section is a warm-up; it offers puzzles that are challenging enough for beginning and intermediate puzzle solvers, but are not overly difficult.

The second section is a different story. All of the puzzles in this section are difficult and, in some cases, very difficult. It was created for the best of puzzle solvers world-wide. Neither section requires mathematics beyond first semester algebra for solutions.

Interspersed throughout both sections are word puzzles called *Thinkerobics*, where the puzzle solver is required to come up with a well-known phrase by solving the riddle posed by the placement of the letters and figures inside the box.

When Ruth Cavin, my editor at St. Martin's, and I first discussed this book, I proposed a book composed entirely of the most difficult puzzles imaginable. I told Ruth that, from the letters I received from puzzle fans about my previous books, it was clear that there were two groups of readers: those that relished the difficult puzzles and those who enjoyed the moderately difficult math puzzles and the word puzzles. In the latter category, most of the letters came from young people and beginning puzzle solvers. Ruth immediately suggested a combination book that would offer something for everyone....

We both agreed that there were too many puzzle books on the market that were rehashes of old classics. Because of this, every effort was made to design each puzzle with a fresh approach. We hope you will let us know if we accomplished this. As an example, you will notice several "quickie" puzzles in the second section that may require some research. There is enough information to give you a general idea of what the question requires for its solution. The twist is, you may have to do a little digging to come up with the answer. There are additional mind treats that I will let you discover on your own.

A special thanks is in order to my friend and colleague, Linda McGlaughlin. Linda spent countless hours helping me to fine-tune this book. Without her efforts, this book would have never come into being.

The ultimate purpose of this collection is for you to have fun...PERIOD! I hope you have as much fun solving these puzzles as I had creating them.

Good luck in your puzzle-solving adventures....You'll need it for the second section, especially.

Are You as Smart as You Think?

Part One

WARM-UPS

Answers start on page 29

1.   A box of candy can be divided equally (without cutting pieces) among 2, 3, or 7 people. What is the least number of pieces of candy the box could contain?

2.   *Anagrams* are new words created from the letters of another word. For example, one anagram of the word EVIL is LIVE; another is VILE. Another example is STARCH, which has an anagram in the word CHARTS. Below are five words. See if you can come up with at least one anagram for each one. It might be fun to do this with some friends and make a game to see who can come up with anagrams the fastest!

   1. MILES
   2. GREASE
   3. HORNETS
   4. SCREAM
   5. TRAINS

3.   **Thinkerobics**

    Y R
    – communications
    _____

---

4.   Below is a list of scores from a fictitious college basket-
     ball season. Based on the given scores only, if Kansas
     State were to play Tulane during this particular season,
     who would win and by how much?

Tulane	83	New Mexico	69
Kansas State	93	Northern Iowa	92
New Mexico	95	Northwestern	91
Northern Iowa	101	California	98
Northwestern	62	Boston College	59
California	79	Minnesota	75
Minnesota	88	Boston College	56

5.   What four-letter word inserted in the blanks below will
     create four new words from those on either side? *Example:*

MAIL _____ KIND
         MAN

FIRST _____ SHAKE

BACK _____ STAND

6.   Thinkerobics

1. Blood

2. Bat

3. Transylvania

4. Cape

5. Fangs

6. Coffin

7.   A certain logic has been followed in placing the numbers in the circles below. Complete the last circle using the same logical progression.

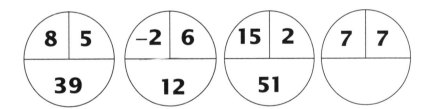

8. There are five books side by side on a shelf. Their colors are gold, orange, brown, pink, and gray. The following information is known about the order of the books:

1. The orange book is between the gray book and the pink book.

2. The gold book is not first and the pink book is not last.

3. The brown book is separated from the pink book by two books.

A. What is the position of the gold book?

B. If the gold book is not next to the brown book, what is the order from first to last of the five books?

9.   Thinkerobics

10. Below is a grid where a certain logic has been established to help you put the missing number in the empty box. What is the missing number?

3	8	7	4	5	9
4	4	4	6	8	7
8	3	2	1	4	

11. To find a common nine-letter word, unscramble the letters below and supply the missing letter in the blank square.

C	N	E
L		F
E	N	I

12. **Thinkerobics**

$$\frac{\text{BOUND}}{-MC^2}$$

13. Below are three sequence puzzles. Can you determine a pattern in each puzzle that will result in continuing the sequence one more step?

A.   0   3   7   10   14   17   21 ____

B.   3   8   14   21   29   38 ____

C.   0   5   8   17   24   37 ____

14. The letters below are arranged in a certain pattern to form a phrase of several words. What is the missing letter and what is the resulting phrase?

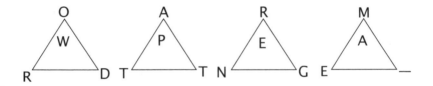

15. **Thinkerobics**

> **Ag NNIVERSARY**

16. Below is a grid with four symbols having four different whole number values. No number is greater than 6. Each line adds up to the number at its end. Can you find the value for each symbol? And the number 19 in the corner is the sum of the diagonal.

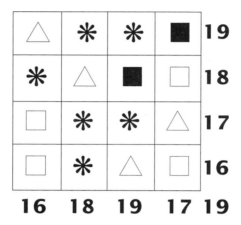

17. The words listed below have an unusual feature. Can you identify that feature? Do you know its name?

RADAR   REFER   LEVEL   CIVIC   SOLOS

18. Thinkerobics

19. Of the words listed below, one is the "odd one out." Can you find the word and the reason it shouldn't be included with the rest? *HINT:* Don't consider parts of speech, vowels, consonants, or syllables.

DEFINE   ABCESS   HIJACK   STUDY   NORTH

20. Most of us know that a young dog is a pup, that a young rabbit is a bunny, and that a young deer is a fawn. Can you match the animals in the left column with the appropriate name of their young in the right column?

1. SWAN   **A. JOEY**
2. GOAT   **B. FINGERLING**
3. FROG   **C. KID**
4. KANGAROO   **D. CYGNET**
5. FISH   **E. POLLIWOG**

21. Thinkerobics

22. In the addition below, what is the least number of digits that would have to be changed to make the total 196?

```
 61
 96
 18
───
175
```

23. Eighteen is ½ of 36. Thirty-six is ¼ of 144. One hundred forty-four is ¼ of 576. What is 144 divided by ½?

24. Thinkerobics

25. Below are five versions of an unfolded cube. One of the five choices is impossible. Which one?

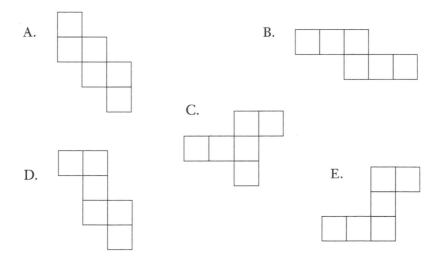

26. What four-letter word can be placed in front of each of the following words to make five new words?

_____ **LAND**

_____ **LINE**

_____ **SAIL**

_____ **STREAM**

_____ **STAY**

27. Thinkerobics

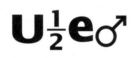

28. How many squares of any size can be found in the figure below?

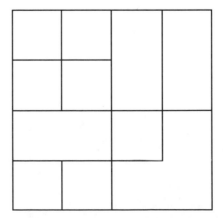

29. What is the next letter in the following sequence?

J   J   A   S   O   N   D   __

30. **Thinkerobics**

> **often**
> **often**
> **often not**
> **often**
> **often**
> **often**

31. Below are three grids. See if you can determine the logic to fill in the fourth grid.

32. Below are five analogies in which you must fill in the blank so that the second pair in the statement has the same relationship as the first pair. You may not know the answer right away, but if you can figure out what the relationship is in the first pair, you shouldn't have much trouble.

    A. *Centimeter* is to *Meter* as *1 yard* is to ___ yards.

    B. *Bear* is to *Mammal* as *Turtle* is to ___.

    C. *$* is to *Dollars* as *£* is to ___.

    D. *Left-to-right* is to *Slice* as *Right-to-left* is to ___.

    E. *3, 6, 9* is to *9, 36, 81* as *2, 4, 8* is to ___.

33. Thinkerobics

34. While skiing, Martha took a dare . . . and ended up in a cast.

DARE

_____

_____

_____

CAST

By changing one letter at a time, beginning with _DARE_ can you come up with three words that will lead you to _CAST_? I'll give you one solution in the answer section, but you may find a different one that will lead you to _CAST_. And that's okay as long as you change one letter at a time.

35. All the words listed below share a common feature. What is it?

EVIL	**POTS**
BATS	**SPOOL**
REWARD	**TIME**

36. **Thinkerobics**

37. If we count by 3s, starting with 1, the sequence begins like this:

1, 4, 7, 10, 13, 16 . . .

What is the fiftieth number in this sequence?

38. Below is a grid of sixteen dots. What is the maximum number of straight lines you can draw between the dots without lifting your pencil and without crossing any lines you may have already drawn? Any line connecting two dots counts as one individual line. Use only horizontal and vertical lines.

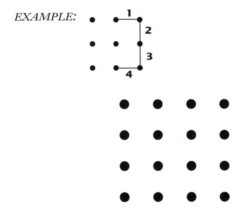

39. **Thinkerobics**

TRIPwinLE
————————
time

40. Fill in the missing numbers for each of the four blanks below. Be careful. One of the answers may require another point of view!

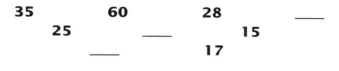

HINT: One of the blanks can be filled in with one of *two* possible numbers.

41. Using all the whole numbers 0 through 9, used only once each, there are several ways to arrive at a sum total of 100. One way is $0 + 1 + 2 + 3 + 4 + 6 + 7 + (8 \times 9) = 100$. Another way is $97\,^{43}\!/_{86} + 2\,^{5}\!/_{10}$. Can you come up with at least one other way?

42. Thinkerobics

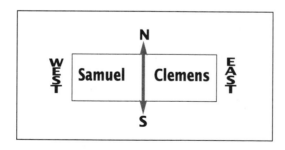

43. Roman numerals are fun to explore every now and then. Here's a challenge for you. Can you write 948 in Roman numerals? *HINT:* There are eight different characters in the answer.

44. Below is a grid composed of sixteen letters that spell a common word. The letters are sequenced in a logical pattern for you to discover and find the word. The circled *E* is the last letter of the word.

N   U   O   C

T   I   W   K

E   S   Ⓔ   C

R   C   L   O

45. Thinkerobics

46. I recently returned from a trip. Today is Tuesday. I returned three days before the day after the day before tomorrow. On what day did I return?

47. One of the figures below lacks a common characteristic that the other five figures have. Which one is it and why?

48. Thinkerobics

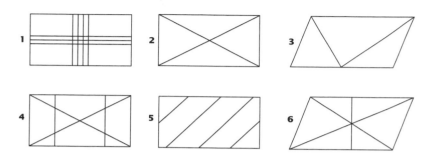

DICT**JURY**MENT

49. How many different words can you create from the letters in the word *NUMBER*? You can use each letter only once in your new words.

50. If you know that the opposite sides of one die always totals the same, what are the numbers on the four faces that are stuck together in the picture below?

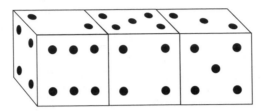

51. **Thinkerobics**

FIN —— ITE

52. Find the words whose initials are on the right side of each equation below and that indicate a list or measurement. (The first answer is shown.)

1. 26   =   **L of the A (Letters of the Alphabet)**

2. 6   =   **S of a C**

3. 2   =   **P in a Q**

4. 60   =   **M in an H**

5. 360   =   **D in a C**

53. At a sports banquet there are one hundred famous athletes. Each one is either a football or basketball player. At least one is a football player. Given any two of the athletes, at least one is a basketball player. How many of the athletes are football players, and how many are basketball players?

54. Thinkerobics

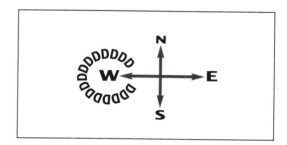

55. Below is an addition puzzle where each letter stands for a digit between 0 and 9. No word can begin with a zero. Can you replace the letters with the correct number to make the addition problem add up correctly?

BOB
BOB
GO
⎯⎯⎯⎯
LOOK

56. I am thinking of a five-digit number where the fifth digit is one-half the fourth digit and one-fourth the third digit. The third digit is one-half the first digit and twice the fourth digit. The second digit is three times the fourth digit and five more than the fifth digit. What is the five-digit number?

57. Thinkerobics

G, I C U R YY 4 me 2 **think**

58. How many triangles of any size are in the configuration below? *HINT:* Look for an easy, systematic approach to count the triangles.

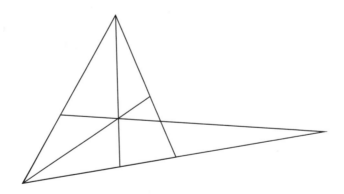

59. Sixty-nine percent of all people are chocolate eaters, and 22 percent of all people are under the age of fifteen. Given that a person has been selected at random, what is the probability that the person is not a chocolate eater and above the age of fifteen?

60. **Thinkerobics**

61. Below is a phrase written in code. It is a motto about life that everyone should consider!

OCMG KV HWP!

62. Here's a "double trickle-down" puzzle. Change one letter at a time in each word for each column and arrive at *FARE*.

MILD   **COLD**

‾‾‾‾‾   ‾‾‾‾‾

‾‾‾‾‾   ‾‾‾‾‾

‾‾‾‾‾   ‾‾‾‾‾

FARE

63. Thinkerobics

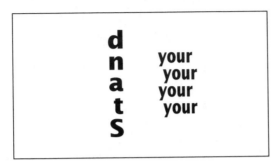

64. What are the next four letters in the sequence below?

J A F E

M A A P

M A J U

J U A U

S E O C

___ ___ ___ ___

65. The numbers below are arranged in a logical manner, but a little different perspective should help you decipher what to put in place of the blank. What is the missing number?

8 1 12 10 14 11 ___ 3 7 5 16 9

66. Thinkerobics

67. Mathematicians love to have specific names for every-thing as well as symbols. For instance, there may be more names for different types of numbers than you ever dreamed possible. *WHOLE*, *NEGATIVE*, *COMPLEX*, and *PRIME* are just a few. How many more names can you find?

68. From *CHERRIES* to *MUSIC*—quickly now, can you come up with an anagram of *MARASCHINO*?

69. Thinkerobics

often often   many many R
──────────────────────────────
looked

70. If ²⁄₁₇ of some number is ¹⁷⁄₄₃ of ⁷⁄₁₉, what is the number expressed as a fraction?

71. What four-letter word will fit in the blank to create two new words from those on either side in each grouping below? Each line will have a different four-letter word.

1. ROAD _____ **BOOK**

2. BEAN _____ **GAME**

3. NICK _____ **LESS**

4. PUSH _____ **LOOK**

72. What is the closest relationship my daughter could have with my sister's nephew's mother's sister?

73. Thinkerobics

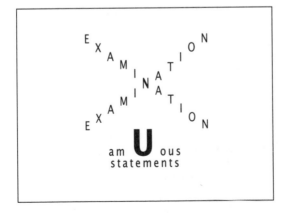

74. Below are four interesting words that may be more than they seem. What makes them more than they appear? *HINT:* Anagrams.

RECALLS

LISTEN

EVIL

TAPES

75. **Thinkerobics**

Part One

WARM-UP
ANSWERS

1.   42. The lowest common denominator of 2, 3, and 7 is
$2 \cdot 3 \cdot 7$ or 42.

2.   1. MILES — SMILE — LIMES — SLIME

2. GREASE — AGREES

3. HORNETS — SHORTEN

4. SCREAM — CREAMS

5. TRAINS — STRAIN

3.   Wireless communications

4.   Kansas State would beat Tulane by 19 points.

A. Minnesota beat Boston College by 32 points and
Northwestern beat Boston College by 3 points. If
Minnesota were to play Northwestern, they would
win by 29 points.

B. New Mexico beat Northwestern by 4 points and since
Minnesota would have beaten Northwestern by 29
points, they would beat New Mexico by 25 points.

C. Tulane beat New Mexico by 14 points, so Minnesota
would beat Tulane by 11 points.

BUT

D. California beat Minnesota by 4 points, so California
would beat Tulane by 15 points.

E. Northern Iowa beat California by 3 points, so Northern Iowa would beat Tulane by 18 points.

F. Finally, Kansas State beat Northern Iowa by 1 point, so Kansas State would beat Tulane by 19 points.

5.   Hand

6.   Count Dracula

7.   42. Add the top two numbers of each circle and multiply by 3 to get the bottom number.

8.   A. Fifth position

B. Brown, gray, orange, pink, gold

9.   Rhodes Scholar

10.   6. This is simply an addition problem.

$$
\begin{array}{r}
387,459 \\
+\ 444,687 \\
\hline
832,146
\end{array}
$$

11.   INFLUENCE. The missing letter is U.

12.   Boundless energy.

13.   A. 24. The differences between the numbers alternates 3, 4, 3, 4, ... So the next response after 21 is 24.

B. 48. Here the differences between the numbers increases by 1, starting with 5 (3 to 8), so the answer is 48 because the difference has to be 10 between 38 and the next number.

C. 48. The pattern looks like this:

$$1^2 - 1, \ 2^2 + 1, \ 3^2 - 1, \ 4^2 + 1, \ 5^2 - 1, \ 6^2 + 1, \ 7^2 - 1$$

14. The missing letter is *s* and the phrase spells out *WORD PATTERN GAMES.*

15. Silver anniversary

16. □ = 3
✳ = 4
■ = 5
△ = 6

A. Look at columns 1 and 4:
△ + ✳ + □ + □ = 16 (column 1)
■ + □ + △ + □ = 17 (column 4)
This shows that ■ has a value of 1 greater than ✳.

B. Now, from column 2 and row 2:
✳ + △ + ✳ + ✳ = 18 (column 2)
✳ + △ + ■ + □ = 18 (row 2)

Therefore, ✳ + ✳ = ■ + □.

Since ■ has a value of 1 greater than ✳, then it must have a value of 2 greater than □.

C. We now know:
■ is 1 greater than ✳, and
■ is 2 greater than □.

D. Now look at column 2:
✳ must be a 4 or a 5 if no number is greater than 6.

E. Consider the possibilities:
If ✳ is a 5, then: △ = 3
□ = 4
✳ = 5
■ = 6

But this is incorrect, since these values make the diagonal total 15 instead of 19.

Therefore,

✳ = 4, □ = 3, ■ = 5, and △ = 6.

17. The words are spelled the same way both forward and backward. Words and numbers that have this feature are called "palindromes."

18. Mad dash for home

19. North. All the other words start with three consecutive letters of the alphabet.

20. 1. D
2. C
3. E
4. A
5. B

21. Mutual bonds

22. None! Or all, depending if you consider turning the three numbers upside down.

$$
\begin{array}{r}
81 \\
96 \\
\underline{19} \\
196
\end{array}
$$

23. 288. Did I fool you? When you divide by a fraction, you invert the fraction and multiply the number by the inversion. In this case, $144 \div \frac{1}{2} = 144 \cdot \frac{2}{1} = 288$.

24. Solid performance

25. E

26. **MAIN** MAINLAND
      MAINSTREAM
      MAINLINE
      MAINSTAY
      MAINSAIL

27. You have e-mail.

28. 15

29. J. These are the first letters of the months of the year starting with June.

30.   More often than not

31.

	O	X	
X	X		
		O	
X		O	X

Turn the first grid 90° clockwise to get the second grid; then, turn 90° clockwise again to get the third grid. One more turn 90° clockwise will give you the answer.

32.   A. *100 yards*

B. *Reptile*

C. *Pounds* (sterling)

D. *Hook* (in golf, the movement of the ball by a right-handed player)

E. *4, 16, 64*

33.   Dead in the water

34.   Here's one way to solve this:

DARE
BARE
BASE
CASE
CAST

35. Each is a different word when spelled backward. Words like these are called "recurrent palindromes."

EVIL — LIVE   POTS — STOP
BATS — STAB   SPOOL — LOOPS
REWARD — DRAWER   TIME — EMIT

36. Misunderstanding between lovers

37. 148. If you look at the sequence, you will see that the formula is $n = 3(p - 1) + 1$, where p is the position. So for 50, $n = 3 \cdot 49 + 1$ or 148. Another way to look at this is to make a chart showing the numbers in the sequence, their position, and the relationship of each number to its position.

Number	1	4	7	10	13	16
Position	1	2	3	4	5	6
Difference	0	2	4	6	8	10

Notice that the difference for the first position is 0; after that, the difference between each respective number and its position increases by 2. To use this pattern to determine the number in any position, multiply by 3 (since that is the difference between each NUMBER in the sequence) the number of the POSITION you are trying to find, then subtract 2, the DIFFERENCE (sequentially or horizontally) between numbers in the *difference* row.

38.   21. Here's one possible solution:

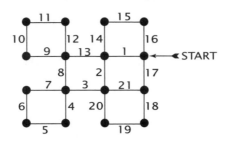

39.   A win in triple overtime

40.   Each blank should contain the difference between the two numbers on each side above it; thus:

1. The number in the first row can be either 43 or 13.

2. The number in the second row is 32.

3. The number in the third row is 7.

4. 10 is the final number.

41.   Here are four other ways. Did you find any of these, or others?

1. $78\frac{5}{6} + 21\frac{45}{90} = 100$ 3. $90 + 8\frac{3}{6} + 1\frac{27}{54} = 100$

2. $89 + 6\frac{1}{2} + 4\frac{35}{70} = 100$ 4. $97\frac{43}{86} + 2\frac{5}{10} = 100$

42.   "East is east and west is west and never the 'twain shall meet."

43. 948 = CMXLVIII

44. Starting with the *C* in the upper right-hand corner and rotating counterclockwise, the word spells COUNTER-CLOCKWISE.

45. It's to die for.

46. Sunday. The day before tomorrow is today (Tuesday); the day after that is Wednesday. Three days before that is Sunday.

47. No. 1. It has only horizontal and vertical lines.

48. Grand jury indictment

49. Here are ten new words. Did you find more?

BURN   NUMB   BUN   RUN   NUB

URN   MEN   RUM   BUM   RUE

50. 3, 6, 1, 6

From the first two dice, you can see that 4 is not opposite 2, 6, or 5. That leaves 1 or 3. It must be 3, because each die has a 6, so the total of opposite faces must be at least 7, which is exactly what the total is. So we know that the first face stuck to the second die is a 3. The second face must be a 1 or a 6. Look at the first die. Imagine spinning the cube around, knowing that the 5 is on the bottom, and facing the 4 out toward the front and eventually twisting the 5 to the top as in the second cube. If you can visualize this movement, then you know the 6 is the second answer and stuck to the 3 of the first die. The third and fourth faces must be a 1 or a 6 or a 6 and a 1. Again, spin the second cube around in your mind's eye to position it as the third cube, and you see that the third face is a 1 and the fourth face is a 6.

51.   Infinite space

52.   2.   6 = *Sides* of a *Cube*

3.   2 = *Pints* in a *Quart*

4.   60 = *Minutes* in an *Hour*

5. 360 = *Degrees* in a *Circle*

53.   Only one of the athletes is a football player. The other ninety-nine are basketball players.

54.   West Indies

55.   757
       757
        45

      1559

56.   86421

57.   Gee, I see you are too wise for me to outthink.

58.   16. One way to approach this is to label all the points where lines intersect (see accompanying diagram). Then, starting alphabetically with AB, record all the triangles that have AB as a side, then AC, AD etc. List your results in columns, and count your total when you've named them all.

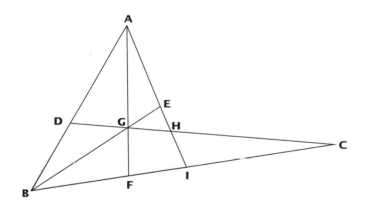

ABE	BCD	CFG	EGH	16 TRIANGLES
ABF	BCG	CHI		
ABI	BDG			
ADG	BEI			
ADH	BFG			
AEG				
AFI				
AGH				

59.   24.18%

Thirty-one percent of all people are not chocolate eaters and 78% of all people are older than fifteen years. Therefore, 31% · 78%, or 24.18%, are neither chocolate eaters nor below the age of fifteen.

60.   Drooping eyelids

61.   The phrase is *MAKE IT FUN!*
Below is the code-breaking chart:

A	B	C	D	E	F	G	H	I	J	K	L	M	N	O	P
1	2	3	4	5	6	7	8	9	10	11	12	13	14	15	16

Q	R	S	T	U	V	W	X	Y	Z
17	18	19	20	21	22	23	24	25	26

Moving the numbering over two places to the left, you get:

A	B	C	D	E	F	G	H	I	J	K	L	M	N	O	P
25	26	1	2	3	4	5	6	7	8	9	10	11	12	13	14

Q	R	S	T	U	V	W	X	Y	Z
15	16	17	18	19	20	21	22	23	24

62.   Here's one way:

```
MILD                    COLD
  MILE                CORD
    FILE            CORE
      FIRE    CARE
        FARE
```

63. Stand up for your rights.

64. NODE. These are the first two letters of the months . . . in order, beginning with JAnuary-FEbruary.

65. 6. Starting with the two outside numbers (8 and 9), and moving toward the middle in this fashion, each pair of numbers totals 17.

66. Expanding waistline

67. Here is a list of some of the other kinds of numbers. Can you find more?

1. rational	12. real
2. integers	13. imaginary
3. trans finite	14. decimal
4. algebraic	15. composite
5. odd	16. positive
6. even	17. transcendental
7. fractions	18. amicable
8. counting	19. figurate
9. irrational	20. perfect
10. cardinal	21. natural
11. ordinal	22. Fibonacci

68. HARMONICAS

69. Too often too many are overlooked.

70. $\dfrac{2,023}{1,634}$

$$\frac{2}{17} \cdot x = \frac{17}{43} \cdot \frac{7}{19}$$

$$\frac{2}{17} \cdot x = \frac{119}{817}$$

$$2x = \frac{119}{817} \cdot 17 = \frac{2,023}{817}$$

$$x = \frac{2,023}{817(2)} = \frac{2,023}{1,634}$$

$$x = \frac{2,023}{1,634}$$

71. 1. WORK

2. BALL

3. NAME

4. OVER

72. She would be my daughter's aunt.

73. Ambiguous statements under cross-examination

74. All have at least two anagrams:

1. RECALLS — CALLERS, CELLARS
2. LISTEN — ENLIST, TINSEL, SILENT, INLETS
3. EVIL — LIVE, VEIL, VILE
4. TAPES — PATES, SPATE

75. Overlapping appointments

Part Two

KILLERS

Answers start on page 83

76. Below are nine sequence puzzles where you are to find the missing number. No higher mathematics are required . . . not even algebra. If you have a pencil and a piece of paper, you have everything you need to solve these!

1. 46,656 3,125 256 27 _____ 1

2. 8 1 22 5 0 6 21 _____

3. 4 2 8 5 7 1 _____

4. –36 –10 8 18 20 14 _____

5. 3 10 7 8 _____ 12 9 16

6. 3 3 7 8 11 13 15 18 19 _____

7. 1 2 4 12 24 52 _____

8. 1 4 9 6 5 6 9 9 4 _____

9. 4 14 4 0 11 23 144 _____

77. Below are five analogy puzzles. Feel free to use any resource to solve these.

1. *Wedge-shaped* is to *cone-shaped* as *cuneiform* is to _____.

2. *Greek* is to *Roman* as *Aphrodite* is to _____.

3. *Probability* is to *odds* as *4 out of 5* is to _____.

4. *Café* is to *store* as *coffee* is to _____.

5. *1* is to *tangent* as *2* is to _____.

78. Thinkerobics

79. What should the last grid look like in the sequence below?

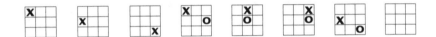

80. Below are five quickies. Find a friend before you look at these. Agree upon a time limit and see who can solve the most puzzles in that time!

A. **What fraction represents 0.75757575 . . . ?**

B. **What does the following number represent?**
   9.42477

C. **Water is to H_2O as Hydrogen peroxide is to _____.**

D. **The incus is a bone that can be found where?**

E. **To what do the following words refer?**
   arc, charge, bank, zone, glass, baseline

81. Thinkerobics

```
FresHEman  himself
```

82. Below is an infinite sequence:

3   11   19   27   35   43   51   59   67   . . .

A. What is a general formula that will give you the number of any position in this sequence?

B. What is the thirty-seventh number in this sequence?

Let n equal the position of the number, e.g., in the case above, $n = 37$.

83. Each circle below has a value somewhere between and including 1 through 9. No two circles have the same value. The four numbers given at the intersections of the circles are the sums of the values of those respective circles. Find the values for the first six circles that are marked with a question mark as well as the value of the intersection of the three circles at the bottom. *NOTE:* No two circles can have the same value.

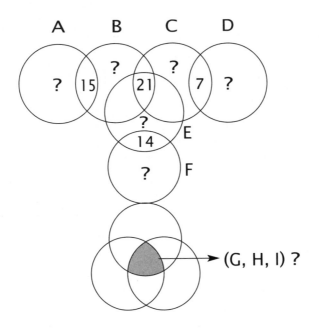

84. Thinkerobics

RISING^{occasion}

85. The NCAA college basketball tournament has been a huge success since they went to the format of selecting a sixty-four-team field. The tournament is a single-elimination tournament with no byes. In all, there is a total of sixty-three games played. If the tournament were to go to a thirty-two-team field and institute a double-elimination format (each team would be disqualified after two losses), what are the maximum number of games that could be played?

86. A group of friends stopped by a local pub for some refreshments. They decided to put charges on one bill. After a short time, two of the friends had to leave in a hurry and didn't leave their portion of the bill. The total of the bill was $63. One of the group told the others, "Everyone throw in two dollars extra and we'll have the bill covered exactly." How many people were originally in the group? It's not that difficult to "intuit" the answer, so the challenge of this puzzle is to defend your answer by demonstrating proof mathematically.

87. Thinkerobics

DAY DAY DAY DAY DAY
CAST CAST CAST CAST

88. Below is a mathematical sequence puzzle.

     0   4   18   48   100   180   _____

A. What number comes after 180?

B. What is the tenth term of this sequence?

C. What is the formula using n as the number of the term that fits this sequence?

89. The total number of Ping-Pong™ balls in a pile like the one shown below (a tetrahedron) is found by the formula,

$$y = \tfrac{1}{6}x^3 + \tfrac{1}{2}x^2 + \tfrac{1}{3}x$$

where x is the number of layers and y is the total number of Ping-Pong™ balls. What would the formula be if the stack consisted of layers of squared numbers of Ping-Pong balls, i.e.,

1, 4, 9, 16, 25 . . . ?

NOTE: Have heart! The formula isn't that much different than the one given above.

(This is the figure at left as viewed from the top.)

90. **Thinkerobics**

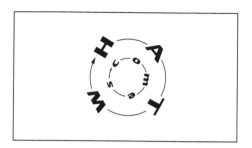

91. Below is a sequence puzzle with a different twist: Even though there are decimals in the sequence, the application that lies behind the puzzle involves whole numbers.

   4   7.5   8.66   84.25   87.6   _____

92. Here are five more quickies. Set a time limit with a friend, or a group, and see who gets the most correct answers in the shortest time.

   A. *100* is to *century* as *300* is to _____ .

   B. *Sri Lanka* is to *Ceylon* as *Taiwan* is to _____ .

   C. *3.1416* is to π as *1.61803* is to _____ .

   D. *Cow* is to *bovine* as *rabbit* is to _____ .

   E. *Time/item* is to *anagram* as *civic/civic* is to _____ .

93. Thinkerobics

```
E    E
P    P
O    O
C    C
S    S
```

94. Cube Eaters from the Fourth Dimension are attacking a stack of sixty-four sugar cubes. A team of Cube Eaters consists of several "face attackers." They enter the cubes from one of the side faces and eat all of the cubes in that row. If they happen to meet one of their teammates eating a row from another face, whoever gets to the cube first gets to eat that cube, and the other one continues on its path. Each Cube Eater team has one "Diagonal Attacker" who starts at the top left corner and eats diagonally through the stack, one cube at a time, to the bottom of the right corner (from A to B in the figure below). How many cubes has this team of Cube Eaters eaten from the stack of sugar cubes shown in the following picture?

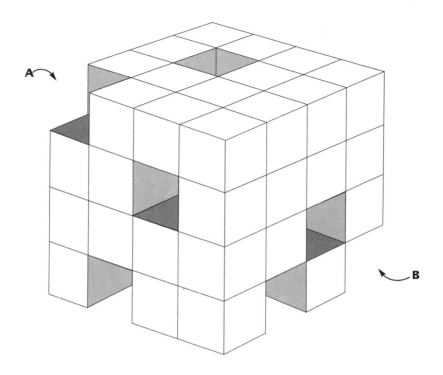

95. What is the sum of the infinite series

$$\frac{1}{7} + \frac{1}{49} + \frac{1}{343} + \frac{1}{2,401} + \frac{1}{16,807} \cdots$$

96. Thinkerobic

97. Here's a neat puzzle: What is the maximum number of straight lines you can draw between the dots below without lifting your pencil? Any line connecting two dots counts as one individual line. Use only horizontal and vertical lines.

Example:

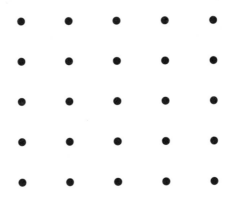

The above drawing represents six lines. The answer for a 3 × 3 grid is ten maximum lines. What is the answer for a 5 × 5 grid? You might be surprised at what you find!

98. Match the words in the left-hand column with the words in the right-hand column. That's all there is to it!

1. FUSIFORM	A. SPUR-SHAPED
2. CLAVIFORM	B. AX-SHAPED
3. CALCIFORM	C. SPINDLE-SHAPED
4. FUNIFORM	D. CYGNET
5. DOLABRIFORM	E. POLLIWOG

99. Thinkerobics

YcOuUrRrHeOnMtE

100. A few more vocabulary quickies for your consideration:

A. You may know that the word for "loss of smell" is *anosmia* and that the word for "loss of sight" is *amaurosis*. What is the word for "loss of taste"?

B. "Skillful with both hands" is to *ambidextrous* as "unskillful with both hands" is to _____

C. To what do the following terms refer?

sinusoidal   isarithm   nachuring   conformal representative fraction

D. The Greek prefix for *blood* is *hemo*. The Latin term is _____.

E. The hardness of minerals is measured on the _____ scale.

101. Here's your mission: Someone has asked you to bring them exactly two gallons of water from an outdoor pump at a cabin. The problem is that there are only two buckets in which to transport the water back to the cabin. One bucket holds thirteen gallons and the other holds seven gallons. Both are made from metal and are heavy even when empty. Your job is to have exactly two gallons of water, placed into the seven-gallon bucket, so that you can carry it back to the cabin. Can this be accomplished? If so, what is the quickest way to do it? Both buckets are empty when you start.

102. Thinkerobics

103. There is an old puzzle that asks you how many revolutions one penny can make around another, stationary penny, as shown below.

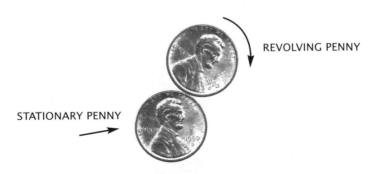

REVOLVING PENNY

STATIONARY PENNY

The answer is that the penny makes two complete revolutions.

Here's the new puzzle: How many revolutions will one penny make around three stationary pennies that are fixed in a row (edge to edge)?

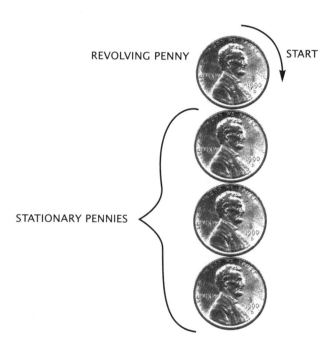

REVOLVING PENNY   START

STATIONARY PENNIES

104. When the proper weights are assigned, the mobile shown here is in perfect balance. What are the three missing weights?

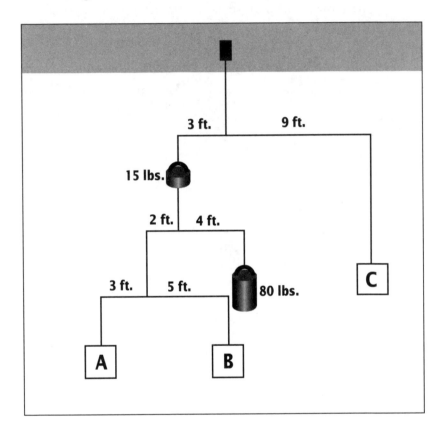

105. **Thinkerobics**

FOOT 12"

106. Cubes can be unraveled in eleven different ways. Below, on the left, is an unraveled cube with symbols on all six faces. On the right is an unraveled cube with a different orientation. Only one of the faces has a symbol that corresponds directly with the cube on the left. Can you fill in the remaining five faces so that when both cubes are put back together they will be identical?

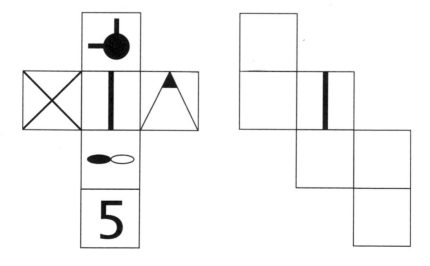

107. Below are five views of stacked cubes that have been fused together. The individual cubes are identical. Can you determine what the sixth view looks like and sketch an orthographic view of the entire stack?

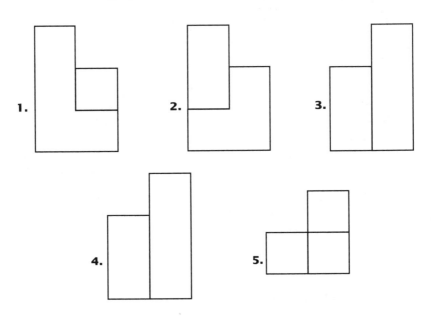

108. **Thinkerobics**

dark darker darkest DAWN
darker dark darkest DAWN
light **dark darkest** DAWN
darker darkest DAWN

109. Below is a double-tiered cardboard configuration that is closed. (The configuration is shown here as transparent for easier viewing.)

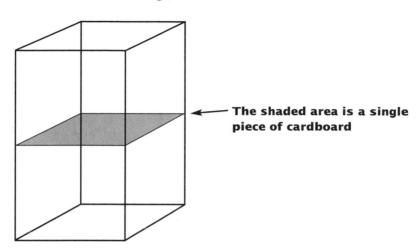

← The shaded area is a single piece of cardboard

Which one of the following choices is a valid depiction of this configuration if it were to be "disassembled" enough to lie flat?

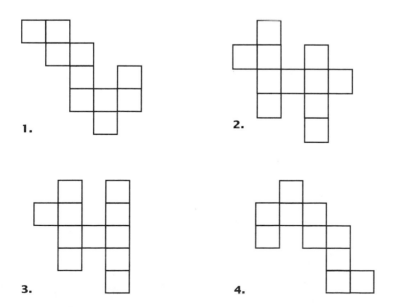

1.

2.

3.

4.

110. Below is the beginning of a pyramid of white and black circles. Can you complete the first three rows?

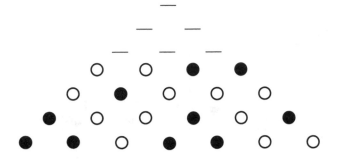

111. Thinkerobics

$$\sqrt{2} \; \pi \; e^{\sqrt{3}}$$
fears

112. Most of us have seen the "9-dot" puzzle, where nine dots are arranged in a 3×3 square and you are asked to connect all nine dots with the fewest number of lines. The answer is that this may be accomplished with four straight lines as follows:

What is the fewest number of lines needed to connect sixteen dots arranged in a 4× 4 square?

113. Below are three polygons with diagonals drawn in each.
The total number of diagonals for each figure is given
below the figure. How many diagonals would a polygon
of twelve sides have? Is there a general formula that will
give you the total number of diagonals in any polygon?
Let n equal the number of sides.

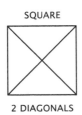

SQUARE

2 DIAGONALS

HEXAGON

9 DIAGONALS

PENTAGON

5 DIAGONALS

114. **Thinkerobics**

115. In the grid below, each symbol represents a digit 1 through 9. The sums of each row and column are given. What is the value of each symbol?

Z	Y	✚	☆	22
◆	X	Y	▲	24
W	☆	▲	✔	23
X	✔	◆	✚	15

15　28　19　22

116. Below is an interesting analogy puzzle. What should the missing figure look like?

```
BBBBBB      CCCCC          D
B             C            D
BBBBB  is to  C    as      D    is to   ?
B             C            D
B             C            D
B           CCCCC        DDDDD
```

117. Thinkerobics

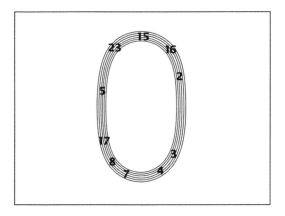

118. The numbers in the right column are related to the respective numbers in the left column. What are the relationships?

1. 3 $\longrightarrow$ 1.31607

2. 5 $\longrightarrow$ 120

3. 7 $\longrightarrow$ 900

4. 11 $\longrightarrow$ 161051

5. 13 $\longrightarrow$ 0.076923

119. At a classic car auction, thirty buyers were present. Ten of the buyers bought fewer than 6 cars. Eight of the buyers bought more than 7 cars. Five buyers bought more than 8 cars. One buyer bought more than 9 cars. What is the total number of buyers who bought 6, 7, 8, or 9 cars?

120. **Thinkerobics**

ROADS, ROADS, ROADS, ROME, ROME

---

121. Below are three columns of words. Each column contains words that share a common characteristic with the other words in that column. Each column has a different characteristic, but all three columns are related under a more global category. What is the characteristic for each column and what is the unifying theme of all three? *HINT:* A clue is given by the horizontal relationship of the words.

AUDITORIUM	BLUEPRINT	ACOUSTICS
TUNNEL	TRIANGLE	PERSPECTIVE
SCULPTURE	ELLIPSE	ESTHETICS
ISLAND	MAP	DISTANCE
GARDEN	MENU	TASTE
ORCHESTRA	NOTATION	CRESCENDO

122. A chemical distribution company sells rare compounds to research labs. One such compound may be purchased at $30 for ⅟₆₀ oz. or $60 for ⅟₃₀ oz. Many of the labs complained that 1/60 oz. was too little and ⅟₃₀ oz. was too much of the compound. An enterprising start-up company then came up with ¼₅ oz. of the same compound for $45. Unfortunately, this company was forced out of business after one year. Can you offer any guesses as to why?

123. Thinkerobics

124. There is an old puzzle that asks you to take four squares of the same size and, using these and only these, create five squares the same size as one of the original squares. The answer is that the fifth square is the "white space" in the middle of the four squares when they touch each other like this:

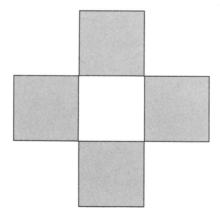

Here's the newest version: Using three squares of the same size, create four squares, each the same size as one of the original three. *HINT:* Think of components and be flexible.

125. Here are five quickies:

1. If a particular system is based on the number 10, we often refer to this system as "decimal." What do we call a system based on the number 20?

2. A group or flock of crows goes by another name. What is it?

3. Can you give an example of an *ananym?*

4. If a basketball player has the combination of more than 9 assists, points, and rebounds in a game, he or she is said to have accomplished a _____ .

5. What does the word *allochthonous* mean?

126. Thinkerobics

```
                    scheme
                scheme scheme
            scheme scheme scheme
        scheme scheme scheme scheme
     scheme scheme scheme scheme scheme
  scheme scheme scheme scheme scheme scheme
```

127. An artist has been hired by an advertising agency to create a display for a grand opening. The head of the agency has told the artist that she needs the display to feature colored, transparent planes of glass intersecting each other to connect to seven points arranged in some global fashion. The agency wants the maximum number of different planes possible. If a plane is determined by three different points, how many planes will the artist have to construct?

128. Of seven people chosen at random, what is the possibility that one or more was born on a Sunday?

129. Thinkerobics

AuLBUM

130. (1) Multiply 50 by 50 one thousand times. (2) Multiply 100 by 100 five hundred times. How many times would you have to multiply the result of (2) to get (1)?

A. One billion times

B. 50 to the 10th power

C. 25 by 25 five hundred times

D. 100 by 100 one thousand times

E. 2.5 to the 25th power

131. Can you write 33,833 in Roman numerals?

132. Thinkerobics

133. **A.** *Cubism* is to *Georges Braque* as *Pointillism* is to _____ .

B. *Served with natural juices* is to *au jus* as *sprinkled with bread crumbs and/or cheese* is to _____

C. *O* is to — — — as *S* is to _____ .

D. *Stamps* are to *philately* as *coins* are to _____ .

E. *Highest peak in Africa* is to *Kibo* as *highest peak in Europe* is to _____ .

134. What is the maximum number of sections resulting when four rectangles are placed one on top of the other? A section is an area that is bound by any of the lines of the rectangles. Below is an example of three rectangles with thirteen sections (not a maximum number for three rectangles).

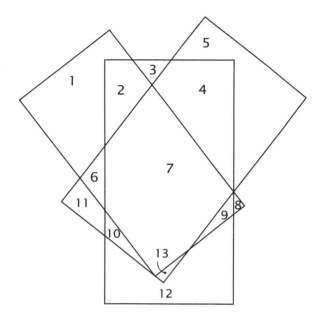

135. **Thinkerobics**

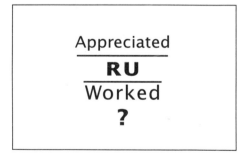

136. Three-tenths of all men in a certain location are married. Two-fifths of all the women in the same location are married. What fraction of this group is single men?

137. Below is an equation where you are asked to solve for an integer x. Although it may appear harmless, very few people can solve it. The beauty of this puzzle is not so much in the answer, but in how you set up the problem to reach the solution.

$$x^{1/3} - x^{1/9} = 60$$

138. Thinkerobics

DRACULA
―――――――
DRAWN

139. Here's a puzzle with a different twist. The twist is that after you come up with an answer, you have to run it by at least three people for their vote of approval. In other words, your solution has to be airtight enough for three or more people, preferably all present when they hear your answer, to give your solution "thumbs up." I have given an answer in the answer section, but it is only one of a myriad possibilities.

A king dies and two men—the only son of the king and an imposter—both claim to be his long-lost son and rightful heir to the throne. Both are identical in looks and appear to be the same age. In a time of war, the queen was sent into hiding to bear this son to protect both her and the newborn prince from the king's enemies. She died shortly after childbirth.

There are no records of the people who raised either man, nor are there birth certificates, school, or other records. The prince knows he is the prince and the imposter knows he is not. The imposter grew up in the hills of a neighboring country hearing the stories about the lost prince and the riches that await upon his return.

An elder of the king's court has a plan to determine the true heir, but it does not involve asking truth-and-liar questions. How did the elder identify the prince?

140. Here are five more quickies for group participation.

1. *Set theory* is to *Georg Cantor* as *group theory is to* _____ .

2. *Yellow* is to *citrine* as *blue* is to _____ .

3. *Causing sleep* is to *soporific* as *causing dormancy* is to _____ .

4. *Handel* is to *Baroque* as *Palestrina* is to _____ .

5. *Piliform* is to *hair-shaped* as *auriform* is to _____ .

141. Thinkerobics

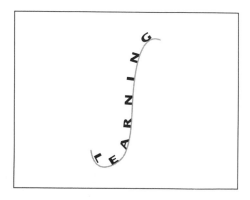

142. Here's a puzzle that seems more confusing than it really is. The object is to match the letters with their respective numbers in accordance with the given clues. Each letter is a different value: 1, 2, 3, or 4.

If A is either 2 or 4, then B is 1.

If A is 3, then B is not 1.

If B is 3, then D is not 2.

If C is 1, then D is not 4.

If C is not 4, then D is 4.

If D is 1, then A is not 2.

143. Below is a cube shown in three different perspectives. Each face contains one of four different symbols. What symbols are on the faces indicated by Arrows #1 and #2? Is there more than one possibility?

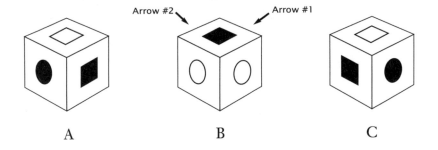

A   B   C

144. **Thinkerobics**

RANK
RANK
RANK
RANK
RANK
RANK
RANK
RANK

145. In the land of Nonnon, the number system resembles ours in the symbols they use for the numbers, but the results of their math operations are different. For instance, $6 \cdot 4 = 26$, $6 \cdot 5 = 33$, and $5 \cdot 7 = 38$. What does $4 \cdot 5 \cdot 6$ equal in Nonnon's number system?

146. You are playing a game of craps, and you've just rolled the dice on your come-out roll . . . and the dice total 5. You're a winner if you roll another 5 before you roll a 7. If you roll a 7 before you roll a 5, you lose. If you roll any other combination before you roll a 5 or a 7, you roll the dice again. With a come-out roll of 5, what are the chances that you will be a winner? You are using two normal dice with six faces on each, numbered 1 through 6.

147. Thinkerobics

$$2'' \times 4'' \text{ Two by six}$$
$$\text{Two by ten } 2'' \times 8'' \; !$$
$$2'' \times 12'' \quad \blacksquare$$

148. In a lab experiment, researchers needed to develop a new temperature scale. This new scale, called Trident, had a freezing point of 20° and a boiling point of 80°. They were also going to be required to convert Trident temperatures into Fahrenheit and Centigrade temperatures. Using "T" as the symbol for the Trident scale, can you express 1. Centigrade degrees and 2. Fahrenheit degrees in terms of T in a general formula? 3. At what point on the Trident and Centigrade scales do they share the exact same numerical temperature? 4. At what point on all 3 scales is the same numerical temperature shared? The conversion formula for Centigrade and Fahrenheit is $F = \frac{9}{5}C + 32$ or $C = \frac{5}{9}(F - 32)$.

149. If ⅓ of ½ = ⅙, what is ⅓ of ½?

150. **Thinkerobics**

2 ^{1}₁^{1}₁

ST   OCK

Part Two

KILLER ANSWERS

76. 1. 4. Expressed in a different form, this puzzle looks like this:

$$6^6 \quad 5^5 \quad 4^4 \quad 3^3 \quad 2^2 \quad 1^1$$

2. 14. This is a sequence where letters of the alphabet correspond directly with the counting numbers where A = 1, B = 2, C = 3, etc., and 0 = Word Space. The phrase spells *HAVE FUN*.

3. 4. This is the fraction ⅘ expressed in decimal form.

4. 0. Take the differences of the numbers and you'll see a pattern develop that will give you the next number:

5. 11. Working from the outside numbers and moving toward the middle, each pair adds up to 19:

$$3, 16 \quad 10, 9 \quad 7, 12 \quad 8, 11$$

6. 23. This is actually two different sequences. Looking at the first 3 and considering every *other* number, the sequence increases by 4: 3, 7, 11, 15, and 19. Looking at the *second* 3 and considering every other number, the series increases by 5: 3, 8, 13, 23.

7. 144. This is the sequence 1, 2, 4, 8, 16, 32, and 64 in our number system of Base$_{10}$ converted to Base$_6$.

8. 1. These are the last digits of the squares of the counting numbers beginning with 1.

9. 1. These are the answers, in consecutive order, of the first eight sequence puzzles!

77. 1. *Piniform* is the word used to describe cone-shaped.

2. *Venus* is the Roman name for Aphrodite.

3. *1 to 4.* Probability is the chance that an event will happen; the odds are determined by comparing the ratio of losses to wins. In this case, it is 1 out of 5 compared to 4 out of 5, or 1 to 4.

4. *Shade* or *blind. Café* is the French word for *coffee*; likewise, *store* is the French word for blind or shade.

5. *Secant.* A tangent intersects a circle at one point; a secant intersects a circle at two points.

78. Chain of fools

79.

O	**X**	

Imagine that each box is numbered as follows:

1	2	3
4	5	6
7	8	9

Starting with the first box and continuing in sequence are the squares of the first 9 numbers: 1, 4, 9, 16, 25, 36, 49, 64. The *X*s represent the first digit, the *O*s represent the second digit of each respective square.

80. A. $^{75}/_{99}$ or $^{25}/_{33}$

B. 3 times π (3 · 3.14159265)

C. H_2O_2

D. The middle ear; also called the "anvil"

E. Basketball

81. He is in a class by himself.

82. A. 291

B. The formula is $8n - 5$.

83. A = 7, B = 8, C = 4, D = 3, E = 9, and F = 5.

The sum of the intersections of the three circles at the bottom is 9.

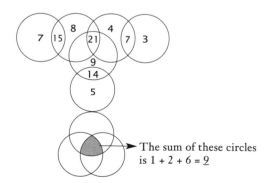

The sum of these circles is $1 + 2 + 6 = \underline{9}$

84.   Rising to the occasion

85.   Sixty-three games. The maximum number of games will be twice the number of entries minus one.

86.   9 people. One way to solve this is by simple algebra.

Let x = the number of people who were initially going to divide the $63-bill evenly.

Let y = the amount of payment owed per person.

Then, $x-2$ = the number of people left to pay, and $y + \$2$ = the amount each of them paid.

We know that

$$\frac{63}{x} = y$$

and we know that

$$x \cdot y = (x-2) \cdot (y+2)$$

so,

$$x \cdot y = xy + 2x - 2y - 4$$
$$2y = 2x - 4$$

But we already know that $\dfrac{63}{x} = y$, so substitute:

$$2 \cdot \dfrac{63}{x} = 2x - 4$$

$$\dfrac{126}{x} = 2x - 4$$

$$126 = 2x^2 - 4x$$

$$2x^2 - 4x - 126 = 0$$

$$x^2 - 2x - 63 = 0$$

$$(x - 9)(x + 7) = 0$$

$$x = 9 \quad \text{or} \quad x = -7$$

$x = -7$ is not relevant in this case, so

$$x = 9 = \text{the original number of people in the group}$$

$$y = \$7 = \text{the amount owed by each person}$$

$$(x - 2) = 7 \text{ people left to pay } (y + 2) = \$9 \text{ each.}$$

87. Five-day forecast

88.   A. 294

   B. 900

   C. $n^3 - n^2$

89. The formula is the one to find the sum of the squares:

$$y = \tfrac{1}{3}x^3 + \tfrac{1}{2}x^2 + \tfrac{1}{6}x$$

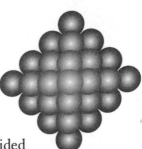

(This is the resulting five-sided
  figure viewed from the top.)

90. What goes around comes around.

91. 89.8333 . . .

The series looks like this:

$$\frac{12}{3} \quad \frac{45}{6} \quad \frac{78}{9} \quad \frac{1011}{12} \quad \frac{1314}{15} \quad \frac{1617}{18}$$

92. A. Tercentenary is a period of 300 years.

B. Formosa. Sri Lanka was formerly known as Ceylon; Taiwan was once Formosa.

C. Ø, the Greek letter "phi." The number 1.61803 is known as the "golden number" or the "golden ratio." The number is actually

$$\frac{(\sqrt{5}+1)}{2}$$

and is the ratio of the $(n + 1)$ term to the nth term as n becomes larger.

D. Leporine

E. Palindrome. A palindrome is a word (or number) that reads the same forward or backward.

93. Up periscope

94. 20

95. ⅙

96. Injury prone

97. 34. Here's one way to do it:

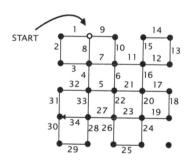

98. 1 — C

2 — E

3 — A

4 — D

5 — B

99. Alternating current in your home

100. A. Ageusia

B. Ambisinistrous

C. Maps or mapmaking

D. Sangui–

E. Mohs'

101. It can be accomplished. Here's one way:

	No. gallons in 13-gal. bucket	No. gallons in 7-gal. bucket
1. Fill the 7-gallon bucket and dump it into 13-gallon bucket.	7	0
2. Repeat. You now are left with 1 gallon in the 7-gallon bucket.	13	1
3. Empty the 13-gallon bucket and pour the 1 gallon from the 7-gallon bucket into it.	1	0
4. Fill the 7-gallon bucket and pour the water into the 13-gallon bucket.	8	0

5. Fill the 7-gallon bucket again and pour into the 13-gallon bucket. Since the 13-gallon bucket will now take only 5 additional gallons $(1+7+5=13)$ you will have 2 gallons in the 7-gallon bucket   13   2

Don't forget to empty the 13-gallon bucket before going back to the cabin.

102. I am out on a limb.

103. Three and a third revolutions. In the diagram below, each numbered penny represents one-third revolution.

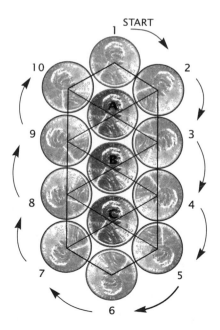

104.   A. 100 lbs.

B. 60 lbs.

C. 85 lbs.

Explanation: On the left side of the mobile, notice the 80-lb.weight is supported through 4-ft. In order for the mobile to balance, this means the 2-ft. segment has to support 160 lbs.

$$80 \text{ lbs.} \cdot 4 = 2 \cdot 160$$

Now that 160 lbs. must be split proportionally into support for a 3-ft. and 5-ft. segment. This is 100 lbs., which is the weight for A, and 60 lbs., which is the weight for B

$$100 \cdot 3 = 60 \cdot 5$$

This means there are 255 lbs. supported by 3 ft. on the left side of the mobile

$$100 + 60 + 80 + 15 = 255$$

In order to balance the right side, the 255 lbs. through 3 ft. has to equal the same number of pounds through 9 ft.

$$3 \text{ ft.} \cdot 255 \text{ lbs.} = 9x$$

$$x = 85 \text{ lbs.}$$

105.   One foot in front of the other

106.

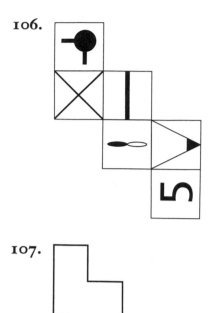

107.

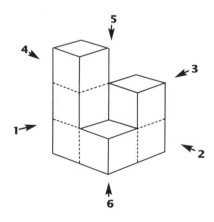

An orthographic view of the cubes:

108. It's always darkest before dawn.

109. No. 2

110.

Starting with the bottom row and moving upward: If two adjacent circles in any row are different from each other (example: ○ ●), then a white circle, ○, goes above and between the two different-colored circles. If two adjacent circles in the same row are the same (example: ○ ○, ● ●), then a black circle, ●, goes above and between the same-colored circles.

111. Irrational fears

112. Six

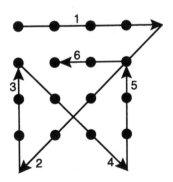

Believe it or not, it cannot be accomplished in less than six lines. There are numerous ways to accomplish this. One way is demonstrated above. (This puzzle was solved by Rob Ellis.)

113. For a twelve-sided polygon there are fifty-four diagonals.

The general formula for the number of diagonals, d, of a polygon on n sides is

$$d = \frac{n^2 - 3n}{2}$$

114. Office space for rent

115. ✚ = 1, **W** = 2, ♦ = 3, **Z** = 4, ✔ = 5, **X** = 6, ▲ = 7, **Y** = 8, and ☆ = 9.

There are several ways to approach this. Below is one:
Look at column 2: **Y**
                       X
                       ☆
                       ✔
                       ‾‾‾
                      28

In order for four numbers between 1 and 9 to total 28, there are only two sets of possibilities:

9   9
8   8
7 or 6
4   5
‾   ‾

Now look at row 4: **X** ✔ ♦ ✚ = 15

The common characters of column 2 and row 4 are ✔ and **X**. Therefore (**Y** + ☆) is 13 more than (♦ + ✚), since

$28 - 15 = 13$. For this to happen, $Y + ☆$ must equal 17, and one symbol must equal 8 and the other 9. This makes $(♦ + ✚) = 4$; and one of these symbols must equal 1 and the other 3. Therefore $(X + ✔) = 11$ (row 4), but we don't know at this point if this is $(7 + 4)$ or $(6 + 5)$.

Now look at column 3 and row 2:

Column 3: ✚   Row 2: ♦ + X + Y + ▲ = 24
            Y
            ▲
            ♦
           ─────
            19

There are three common elements in each:

$$✚ + Y + ▲ + ♦ = 19$$

$$X + Y + ▲ + ♦ = 24$$

$$X - ✚ = 5 \quad (24 - 19)$$

Now go back to where we found $♦ + ✚ = 4$, where the symbols are worth either 3 or 1.

We know that $X - ✚ = 5$, which means that $X = 6$ or 8.

It can't be 8 because we know that either Y or ☆ is 8. Therefore, $X = 6$, which makes $✚ = 1$, $♦ = 3$, and $✔ = 5$.

Now look again at row #2: $♦ + X + Y + ▲ = 24$

We know the value of $♦$ (3) and X (6), which leaves $Y + ▲ = 15$ $(24 - 9)$. We know that the only possibilities for $Y + ▲$ are $9 + 6$ or $8 + 7$. But it can't be $9 + 6$, since $X = 6$. So it is $8 + 7$, where $Y = 8$ and $▲ = 7$. We know this from our first set of possibilities for four numbers to total 28:

```
9        9
8        8
7   or   6
4        5
─        ─
```

Since **X** is in column 2 and we know that it equals 6, **Y** must equal 8. This makes ☆ = 9. Here's what we know:

✛ = 1
♦ = 3
✔ = 5
X = 6
▲ = 7
Y = 8
☆ = 9

We still need to find which symbols represent 2 and 4. Our choices are **Z** and **W**. Look at row 1: **Z** + 8 + 1 + 9 = 22 **Z** must = 4, which makes **W** = 2.

116.

F F F F F
F   F
F F F F F
F   F
F   F
F   F
F   F

(an *R* made up of *F*s)

F is the sixth letter of the alphabet; *I* is the ninth. So *F* is to *I* as 6 is to 9 in the same manner as *L*, which is the twelveth letter, is to *R*, the eighteenth letter.

The smaller letters that make up the larger letters are likewise in a ⅔ ratio. *B* is to *C* as 2 is to 3 in the same manner as *D*, the fourth letter, is to *F*, the sixth letter.

117. Running the numbers

118.   1. 1.31607 is the 4th root of 3.

2. 120 is 5! $(5 \cdot 4 \cdot 3 \cdot 2 \cdot 1)$

3. 900 is the number of degrees in a 7-sided polygon.

4. 161,051 is 11 to the 5th power (11^5).

5. 0.076923 is $\frac{1}{13}$.

119. 19. If ten of the buyers bought less than 6 and one buyer bought more than 9, that means that 11 buyers do not have 6, 7, 8, or 9 cars. That means that the remaining nineteen buyers *do*.

120. "All roads lead to Rome."

121. The first column contains three-dimensional objects; the second column, two-dimensional objects, and the last column, objects of zero (physical) dimensions. The unifying theme is, of course, dimensionality.

122. They were charging approximately 12.5% more than their competition! Although it may appear that $\frac{1}{45}$ oz. for $45 is an equitable midpoint between $\frac{1}{30}$ oz. and $\frac{1}{60}$ oz., it is not. $\frac{1}{45}$ is 0.0222 while the mean of $\frac{1}{60}$ and $\frac{1}{30}$ is 0.02500. The average of the reciprocals of two numbers is different from the reciprocal of the average.

123. The worm turns.

124. Here's one way: Place two 1-inch squares one inch apart from each other:

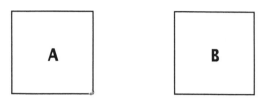

Now "break down" the third square into four equal lines—

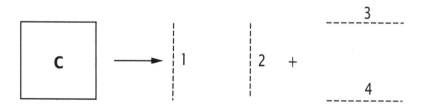

Use the two horizontal lines to cover the top and bottom of the space between "A" and "B," making square C. Place one vertical line in the center of "A" and one in the center of "C." You now have four squares. So they overlap—we didn't say they can't!

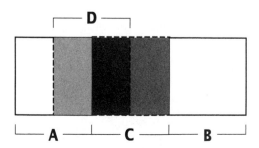

125. 1. Vigesimal

2. A murder of crows

3. The backward spelling of a name, e.g., WILLIAMS—SMAILLIW

4. A "triple-double"

5. Originating elsewhere

126. Pyramid scheme

127. 35. With seven points connected three at a time, and avoiding duplication, the first point can be selected seven different ways; the second, six different ways, and so on. This is expressed as 7! $(7 \cdot 6 \cdot 5 \cdot 4 \cdot 3 \cdot 2 \cdot 1)$. Since three points are to be considered at a time to determine a plane, the first point can be chosen three ways; the second point, two ways, and so on. This is 3! We have to remember that to avoid duplication of points, we must consider 4! ways. The answer looks like this:

$$\frac{7!}{4!3!} = 35 \text{ planes}$$

128. 0.661. The probability of certainty is 1. Six out of the seven can be born on another day of the week; we need only one person born on a Sunday. Since $\left(\dfrac{6}{7}\right)^7$ is the probability that no one was born on a Sunday, to find the answer we need to subtract $\left(\dfrac{6}{7}\right)^{7}$ from 1.

$$1-\left(\dfrac{6}{7}\right)^{7}=0.661$$

129. Gold album

130. C. 25 by 25 five hundred times

131. $\overline{\text{XXXIII}}$ DCCCXXXIII

A bar above a symbol or a group of symbols indicates that the symbol or symbols are to be multiplied by 1,000.

132. Windsor knot

133. 1. *Georges Seurat.* Both artists are generally accepted as the fathers of their respective styles.

2. *Au gratin.* Bread crumbs and/or cheese is acceptable in modern English usage.

3. . . . (Morse Code)

4. *Numismatics*

5. The highest peak in Europe is *Mont Blanc;* the highest in Africa is Kibo. Mont Blanc is in the Alps; Kibo is part of Kilimanjaro.

134. Forty-nine sections

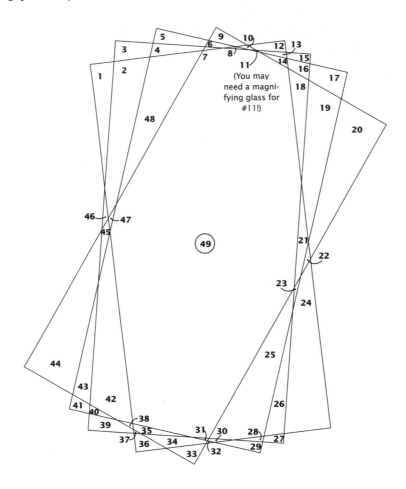

135. Are you underappreciated and overworked?

136. 27½%. There are several ways to approach this. Here's one:

³⁄₁₀ men + ²⁄₅ women = total married

But the number of married men must equal the number of married women. Let's let x=the men and y=the women.

1. $\frac{3}{10}x = \frac{2}{5}y$

2. $x + y = 100\%$

3. Since $\frac{3}{10}x = \frac{2}{5}y$, then $3x = 4y$ and $x = \frac{4}{3}y$

Substituting $\frac{4}{3}y$ for x in equation 2, we have $\frac{4}{3}y + y = 100\%$.

$4y + 3y = 300\%$

$7y = 300\%$

$y = 42\frac{6}{7}\%$

So $42\frac{6}{7}\%$ of the population are women, which means that $57\frac{1}{7}\%$ are men. Since $\frac{3}{10}$ of all men are married, we need to subtract $\frac{3}{10}$ (30%) from $57\frac{1}{7}\%$, finding $27\frac{1}{7}\%$ of the population to be single men.

137. 262,144. Here's one way to approach this:

1. Let $x^{\frac{1}{9}} = y$

2. Let $x = y^9$

3. Then $y^3 - y = 60$

4. $y(y^2 - 1) = 60$

5. $y(y + 1)(y - 1) = 60$

6. From step 5 you can see that three consecutive integers [$(y - 1)$, y, and $(y + 1)$] multiplied together equal 60. The only three numbers that fit are 3, 4, and 5. Therefore, $y = 4$.

7. Now plug step 5 back into step 2 and you get $4^9 = x$ or $x = 262,144$.

8. The cube root of $262,144 = 64$

9. The 9th root of $262,144 = 4$

10. $64 - 4 = 60$, so our answer is correct.

138. Account overdrawn

139. The elder brought both claimants together in a room and said, "For centuries, The Royal Family has taken precautions for such possibilities as we now have. What you don't know is that every Royal Heir has a small Royal Emblem imprinted with indelible ink on the inside of the left buttock at birth. I will give the imposter 30 seconds to tell me he is not the Prince, and if I don't hear from him, I will check for the Royal Emblem. If the imposter does not admit his lie within 30 seconds, he will be killed on the spot once the discovery is made. If the imposter does finally admit he is not the heir, I will give him 1,000 pieces of gold and send him on his way with never a word mentioned about the incident."

The prince, of course, was unfazed by this. The imposter immediately confessed. The elder then told both men that there was no Royal Emblem anywhere on their bodies. He welcomed the Prince home . . . and beheaded the imposter on the spot.

140. 1. Evarist Galois. In mathematics, Georg Cantor is considered the father of set theory; Galois the father of group theory.

2. cerulean

3. torporific

4. Renaissance

5. ear-shaped

141. Learning curve

142. A = 1

B = 3

C = 2

D = 4

143. ❑ and ● are interchangeable at Arrows #1 and #2. Looking at perspectives A and C, we must conclude that there are either two ■s or two ●s on the cube. If there is another ●, it must be opposite the visible ●. Likewise, if there is another ■, it must be opposite the visible ■.

For two ● to be opposite would be inconsistent with perspective B, as there is no way that two ●s could be opposite each other. Therefore, ■ must be the other symbol and opposite the visible ■. Now we know that we have the symbols on the six faces: ○, ○, ■, ■, ❑, and ●.

Since we know the location of each symbol on perspective A, we may unfold the cube with the visible ■ in the middle:

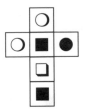

Now unfold perspective B with the ■ on the bottom of the cube being in the middle:

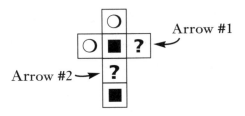

This tells us that ● is at Arrow #1 and ❑ is at Arrow #2.

—OR—

Turning perspective B upside down, you would have the same view: only now, ● is at Arrow #2 and ❑ is at Arrow #1.

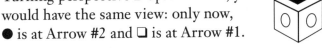

144. Thinning the ranks

145. 143. Their system is based on something other than 10. Let's say it is based on N.

2N + 6 = 26, which is our 24 (4·6). So 2N + 6 = 24; 2N = 18, N = 9. Let's check our 30 (6·5), their 33. 3N + 3 = 30. Again, N = 9. Their number system is based on 9, and 4·5·6, our 120, is their 143.

×	9^2	9^1	9^0
	1	4	3

= 81 + 36 + 3 = 120

146. $\frac{2}{45}$. Your chances of winning are 2 out of 45. After rolling the 5 on the first roll, your chances of rolling a 5 are $\frac{4}{36}$ or 1 out of 9. Out of 36 possible combinations, a 5 can appear four times: 2 + 3, 3 + 2, 1 + 4, or 4 + 1. The chances of rolling a 7 are $\frac{6}{36}$ or 1 out of 6. Out of 36 possible combinations, a 7 can appear six times in this manner: 1 + 6, 6 + 1, 2 + 5, 5 + 2, 3 + 4, or 4 + 3.

Since you can roll a 5 four ways and a 7 six ways, there are a total of 10 ways to roll a 5 or a 7. Four of those ten ways are winning rolls: $\frac{4}{10}$ or $\frac{2}{5}$. This has to be multiplied by the chances of rolling a 5 on your first roll, which is $\frac{1}{9}$. So that $\frac{2}{5} \cdot \frac{1}{9} = \frac{2}{45}$.

147. All aboard!

148. 1. $T = \frac{3}{5}C + 20$

2. $T = \frac{1}{3}F + \frac{28}{3}$

3. 50°

4. There is no common point among the three scales.

1. If you compare the Centigrade and Trident scales, it is readily apparent that there is a 60° difference between the freezing and boiling points on the Trident scale. Likewise, there is a 100° difference between these two points on the Centigrade scale. This means that the Centigrade scale is in a $5/3$ ratio to the Trident scale. Since the Trident scale's freezing point begins at 20° and Centigrade's at 0°, the formula then becomes $T = 3/5C + 20$.

2. For the Fahrenheit scale, find C in the Trident-Centigrade formula:

$$T = 3/5C + 20$$

$$5T = 3C + 100$$

$$3C = 5T - 100$$

$$C = \frac{5T - 100}{3}$$

3. To find the point where the temperatures are the same on the Centigrade and Trident scales ($T = C$), set the formula as follows:

$$T = 3/5T + 20$$

$$5T = 3T + 100$$

$$2T = 100$$

$$T = 50°.$$

Since this is also equal to C, T and C are the same at 50°.

4. If we use the same logic as above to find the common point on the Trident and Fahrenheit scales, you find:

Where T = F: $T = \frac{1}{3}T + \frac{28}{3}$

$$3T = T + 28$$

$$T = 14$$

$$C = -40°$$

So T and F are the same at 14°, and C and T are the same at 50°: There is no commonality of temperatures for all the three scales. (For the record, C and F are the same at −40°.)

149. $\frac{1}{15}$. One way to solve this is to set up a proportion:

1. $\dfrac{\dfrac{1}{3} \cdot \dfrac{1}{7}}{\dfrac{1}{9}} = \dfrac{\dfrac{1}{5} \cdot \dfrac{1}{7}}{x}$

2. $\dfrac{\dfrac{1}{21}}{\dfrac{1}{9}} = \dfrac{\dfrac{1}{35}}{x}$

3. $\dfrac{1}{21}x = \dfrac{1}{315}$

4. $x = \dfrac{21}{315}$

5. $x = \dfrac{1}{15}$

150. Two-for-one stock split